Preface

Iris Folding is a fun and exciting way for all people to make spectacular greeting cards and framed art! This craft, using a simple paper folding technique, is done using a template, cardstock and colored paper strips. Some of the most popular papers used are colored envelopes, gift wrap, origami and scrap-booking papers, and holographic paper. This book is packed with full-sized templates, designed to fit a 5x7 greeting card or frame. It also includes something you won't find in other *Iris Folding* books. You will find instructions on how to make your own templates using a very simple method. There are twelve outlines to help get you started! You will also find pages filled with greetings for placing inside your greeting cards. This could be the only book you'll ever need on *Iris Folding*!

I know you will find that the instructions, patterns and templates in this book are very user friendly. You will have as much fun as I did, making cards and framed art in a variety of colors.

May you enjoy God's favor today! Happy folding!

the Simplicity of
Iris Folding

Bonus Features:

Picture Frame Template

Basic Templates For
Creating Your Own Design

Outline Patterns

Greeting Card Messages

Sarah Decker

First published by Dog Ear Publishing
4010 W. 86th Street, Ste H
Indianapolis, IN 46268
www.dogearpublishing.net

ISBN: 978-159858-427-1
Library of Congress Control Number: applied for

This book is printed on acid-free paper.

Printed in the United States of America

Contents

Material List

65# Card stock, variety of colors
Iris Folding papers (origami sheets, scrap-booking papers,
colored envelopes, wrapping paper)
Holographic paper
Pencil
Cutting mat
Paper cutter
Ruler
Adhesive tape
Double-sided adhesive tape
Masking tape
Hand punches (Fiskars, Paper Craft, Media, EK)
Border punches (Fiskars)
Corner punches
Small craft scissors
Fine tipped black marker
Gold fine tipped pen

Using Templates: Step By Step

Although everything in this book is copyrighted, you have my permission to photo copy the templates, in order to make your patterns. You will need to make two copies. One will be used to make your pattern out of cardstock. The other will be your template, guiding you how to layer your paper strips. The illustrations to the right will walk you through the process of preparing your cardstock for *Iris Folding*.

You will also use these photocopies to make patterns for the other parts of your design. Once the *Iris Folding* is completed, you will put adhesive on the other parts and apply them to the front side of the card, in their appropriate places.

You will find that these templates are designed to use three or four colors. If the pattern calls for four colors - A, B, C and D, you can choose to make A and C the same color, and B and D the same color. In other words, you just took a four color template and made it a two color. I have used a variety of combinations, so that you can see you are not locked in to any set 'rules'. Each template will list the number of colors designed for that template and each number assigned to that color. You will find, in some cases, I used only one color. Let your imagination run wild!

1. Take one of your photocopies and cut out the numbered sections only. These are the areas in which you will apply *Iris Folding*. You are creating an outline used for tracing the design onto cardstock.

2. Trace the outline onto a 4.50 x 6.50 piece of cardstock, centering the design. Cut it out, like you did with the numbered sections. Punch your decorative corners and edges from the front side of your card. Looking at the template, you are viewing the back side.

3. Layer the cardstock cutout on top of the template and secure with masking tape. You are now ready for *Iris Folding* (see the *Iris Folding* instructions).

Iris Folding: Step by Step

Welcome to *Iris Folding! Iris Folding* is a technique in which folded strips of colored paper are layered in a spiral pattern behind an aperture opening of a piece of cardstock. It resembles the iris of an eye or camera.

You'll start by positioning the card, with the aperture cutout, over the *Iris Folding* template, face down. You will be working from the back side of the card. Secure it using masking tape. Choose the colors of papers you intend to use and cut them into 1 x 3 inch strips. You may need to trim them as you are working. Each strip should be a little wider than the aperture opening. Fold a border along one side of each strip, folding towards the back side. Make separate piles of each color, putting them in the order in which you want your design to flow.

Now the FUN begins! Start by taking a strip of Color A and line the folded edge up to the inside edge of number 1. The front of the strip will be facing down. Remember, you are working from the back side of the card. Trim the strip to be a little wider than your opening, and tape both ends to the cardstock.

If you have numbers 1a, 1b, etc., you will layer these one after another, before proceeding to number 2.   Once you have completed number 1, continue to 2 using Color B; then 3 using Color C. Some patterns in this book will have a Color D, starting with number 4. You have now completed one round of your pattern. Repeat these steps (4, 5, 6 etc.) until all of the numbers have been layered. Always remember that you are layering in numerical order. It's similar to a 'paint-by-number' set, but you are using paper.

Follow the instructions on the next page, on how to add the finishing touches to your card.

Congratulations on completing your first handcrafted *Iris Folding* greeting card!

Remember, you are working from the back side. When you are done, turn it over to see the final results of the iris fold. At this time, use your template to make the small heart. Adhere it to the front side of the card. Tape a piece of holographic paper over the back side of the 'iris' opening.

On the backside, run two-sided adhesive tape down all four sides of your iris folded card and apply it to a 5 x 7 card. If you are making a greeting card, your card stock will need to be 10 x 7. You'll fold it in half, creating a 5 x 7 card.

11

Wedding Cake

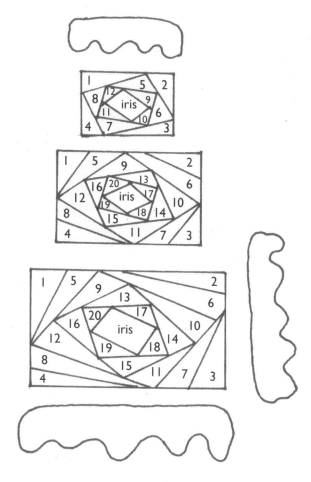

Top Layer:

Color 1: 1, 5, 9

Color 2: 2, 6, 10

Color 3: 3, 7, 11

Color 4: 4, 8, 12

Middle and Bottom Layer:

Color 1: 1, 5, 9, 13, 17

Color 2: 2, 6, 10, 14, 18

Color 3: 3, 7, 11, 15, 19

Color 4: 4, 8, 12, 16, 20

Cut the icing out of cardstock and adhere to the front of the card. Tape a piece of holographic paper over the back side of the 'iris' openings. I chose to use holographic paper on the bottom layer only. On the top two layers, I covered the opening with the same paper I used for the cake. The doves came from the Cross pattern. The flowers were made using a hand punch.

Chef

Color 1: 1a, 1b, 5, 9, 13, 17, 21, 25

Color 2: 2a, 2b, 2c, 2d, 6, 10, 14, 18, 22

Color 3: 3a, 3b, 7, 11, 15, 19, 23

Color 4: 4a, 4b, 8, 12, 16, 20, 24

Start with the hat, layering a, b and c. Complete the remainder of the *Iris Folding*.

Cut out the other pieces and adhere to the front side of the card. Please note that the neck scarf will be applied before the face. The towel will be applied before the hand. Tape a piece of holographic paper over the back side of the 'iris' opening.

Ribbon

This is a pretty simple template. Using only one color, start with number one and continue in numerical order until the *Iris Folding* is complete. This template does not have an 'iris'.

The heart strip was made using a border punch. The tiny hearts and ribbons were made using hand punches.

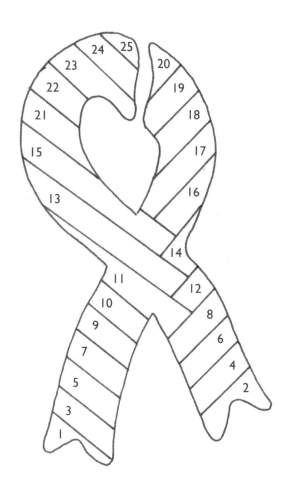

16

Church, School House, Bird House

Color 1: 1, 5, 9, 13, 17, 21

Color 2: 2a, 2b, 6, 10, 14, 18

Color 3: 3a, 3b, 3c, 3d, 7, 11, 15, 19

Color 4: 4a, 4b, 4c, 4d, 8, 12, 16, 20

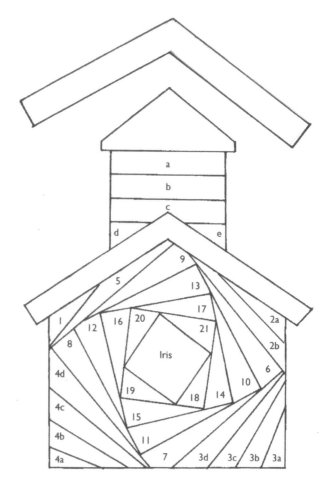

Although this is a four color template, I used only one color. Start with the steeple, completing a, b, c, d and e. Complete the remainder of the *Iris Folding*. Using adhesive, apply the rooftops to the front side of the card. Tape a piece of holographic paper over the back side of the 'iris' opening. If using the iris opening as a photo frame, do not iris fold #'s 18, 19, 20 & 21. Tape your photo over the back side instead of the holographic paper. The bird and alphabets are purchased stickers.

18

Flower Pot

Color 1: 1a, 1b, 1c, 1d, 1e, 5, 9, 13, 17, 21

Color 2: 2a, 2b, 2c, 2d, 6, 10, 14, 18, 22

Color 3: 3a, 3b, 7, 11, 15, 19, 23

Color 4: 4a, 4b, 4c, 8, 12, 16, 20

The starting point on this template is the base of the flower pot. Layer a, b, and c first. After completing the *Iris Folding*, cut the flowers and stems from cardstock and adhere to the front side of the card. Tape a piece of holographic paper over the back side of the 'iris' opening.

Cappuccino Mug

Color 1: 1a, 1b, 1c, 1d, 1e, 9, 12
Color 2: 2a, 2b, 2c, 4, 6, 8, 11, 14
Color 3: 3, 5, 7, 10, 13

Spoon

Color 1: 1, 4, 7
Color 2: 2a, 2b, 2c, 5
Color 3: 3a, 3b, 6

I used one color instead of three.

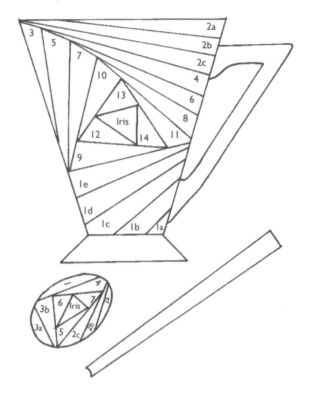

Once the *Iris Folding* is completed, tape a piece of holographic paper over the back side of the 'iris' opening.

Cut the cup handle, cup base and spoon handle out of matching cardstock and adhere to the front of the card.

Get the vine pattern from the Mailbox template.

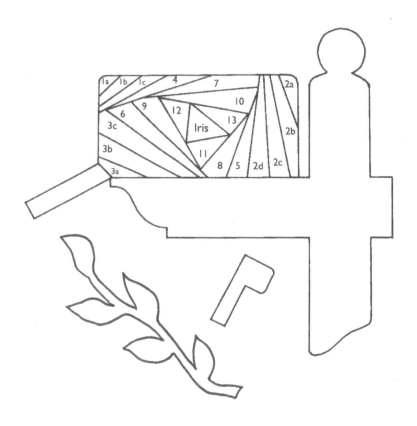

Mailbox

Color 1: 1a, 1b, 1c, 4, 7, 10, 13
Color 2: 2a, 2b, 2c, 2d, 5, 8, 11
Color 3: 3a, 3b, 3c, 6, 9, 12

After completing the *Iris Folding*, cut the mailbox door, post, flag, and vine out of card-stock and adhere to the front of the card. Tape a piece of holographic paper over the back side of the 'iris' opening. There is plenty of room on the post to personalize the mailbox, such as *The Deckers*.

Heart

Color 1: 1a, 1b, 1c, 5, 9, 13, 17, 21, 25

Color 2: 2a, 2b, 2c, 2d, 6, 10, 14, 18, 22

Color 3: 3, 7, 11, 15, 19, 23

Color 4: 4a, 4b, 8, 12, 16, 20, 24

After completing the *Iris Folding*, cut the heart from cardstock and adhere to the front of the card. Tape a piece of holographic paper over the back side of the 'iris' opening.

Balloons

Color 1: 1a, 1b, 1c, 4, 7, 10

Color 2: 2, 5, 8, 11

Color 3: 3a, 3b, 3c, 6, 9, 12

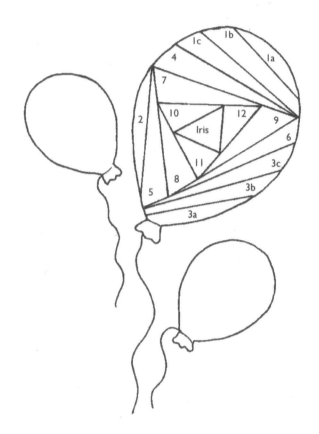

After completing the *Iris Folding*, cut out the small balloons from cardstock and adhere to the front of the card. Tape a piece of holographic paper over the back side if the 'iris' opening. Using a fine tipped black marker, draw the balloon strings.

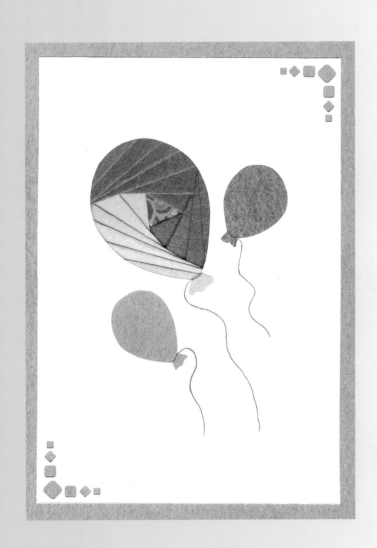

Wine Glass

Color 1: 1, 5, 9, 13, 17, 21

Color 2: 2, 6, 10, 14, 18, 22

Color 3: 3, 7, 11, 15, 19, 23

Color 4: 4, 8, 12, 16, 20, 24

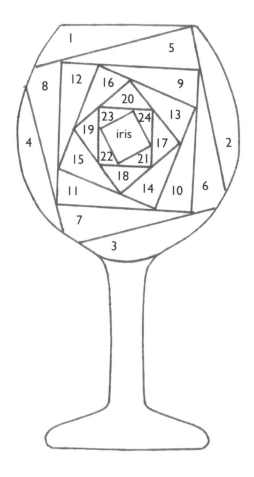

After completing the *Iris Folding*, cut the stem from cardstock and adhere to the front of the card. Tape a piece of holographic paper over the back side if the 'iris' opening. The flowers were made using a hand punch. The green stem was cut out by hand and the wine glass ring was made using circle punches.

Graduation Cap

Color 1: 1a, 1b, 5, 9, 13, 17

Color 2: 2, 6, 10, 14, 18

Color 3: 3, 7, 11, 15, 19

Color 4: 4, 8, 12, 16

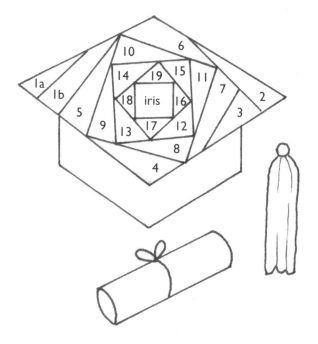

After completing the *Iris Folding*, cut the diploma and tassel out of cardstock and adhere to the front side of the card. Detail it with a black fine tipped marker. Tape a piece of holographic paper to the back side of the 'iris' opening. The stars were made using a hand punch.

Baby Carriage

For the tires, iris fold #'s 1, 2, 3, 4, 5, 6, 7 and 8 using black. Iris fold #'s 9, 10, 11 and 12 using the same color as the carriage.

When doing the carriage top, start with 'a' and continue through 'f'.

After completing the *Iris Folding*, cut the bar, carriage side, ruffle and baby from card-stock and adhere to the front side of the card. Tape a piece of holographic paper over the back side of both 'iris' openings. The carriage side could easily be iris folded by cutting that section out and layering folded strips horizontally, starting at the bottom and working your way to the top. Do it before you do the top of the carriage. After you're finished, apply the ruffle to the front side of the card, using adhesive. The grass and butterflies were made using hand punches.

Present

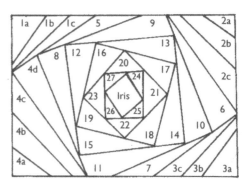

Color 1: 1a, 1b, 1c, 5, 9, 13, 17, 21, 25

Color 2: 2a, 2b, 2c, 6, 10, 14, 18, 22, 26

Color 3: 3a, 3b, 3c, 7, 11, 15, 19, 23, 27

Color 4: 4a, 4b, 4c, 4d, 8, 12, 16, 20, 24

After completing the *Iris Folding*, tape a piece of holographic paper over the back side of the 'iris' opening. Cut the bow out of cardstock and adhere to the front side of the card. The snowflakes and flowers were made using hand punches. The balloons were made using the Balloons pattern.

Birthday Cake

Color 1: 1a, 1b, 1c, 5, 9, 13, 17, 21, 25, 29

Color 2: 2a, 2b, 6, 10, 14, 18, 22, 26, 30

Color 3: 3a, 3b, 3c, 3d, 7, 11, 15, 19, 23, 27

Color 4: 4a, 4b, 4c, 8, 12, 16, 20, 24, 28

The first step to this design is to iris fold the candles (a, b, and c); then begin the *Iris Folding* of the cake. You will start at the top of the candles. Notice that the three candles in the middle will repeat color a.

After completing the *Iris Folding*, tape a piece of holographic paper over the back side of the 'iris' opening. If you wish to tape a photo instead, do not iris fold #'s 23, 24, 25, 26, 27, 28, 29 and 30. Cut the cake plate, flames and icing out of cardstock and adhere to the front side of the card. The squares and circles were made using had punches.

Cell Phone

Color 1: 1, 5, 9, 13, 17, 21

Color 2: 2, 6, 10, 14, 18, 22

Color 3: 3, 7, 11, 15, 19, 23

Color 4: 4, 8, 12, 16, 20, 24

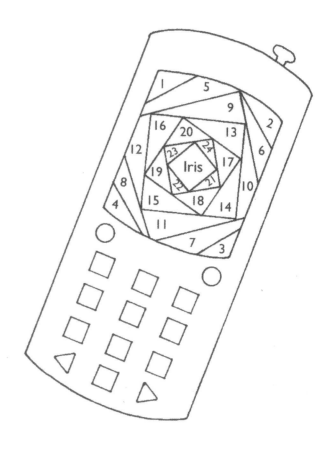

This one is more of a challenge. Cut the cell phone out of cardstock (do not include the antenna). Cut all of the buttons and window out of the cell phone. Cut a piece of cardstock (the color you want for your buttons) to fit over the back side of your cell phone buttons and adhere to the phone (be sure to leave the window open). Using adhesive, adhere the cell phone to your cardstock. Now you will have to cut the window out of the cardstock in order to prepare for *Iris Folding*.

After completing the *Iris Folding*, tape a piece of holographic paper over the back side of the 'iris' opening. If you wish to tape a photo instead, do not iris fold #'s 13, 14, 15, 16, 17, 18, 19, 20, 21, 22, 23, and 24. Cut the antenna out of cardstock and adhere to the front side of the card. The flowers were made using a hand punch.

Lighthouse

Bottom

Color 1: 1a, 1b, 1c, 4, 7, 10

Color 2: 2, 5, 8, 11

Color 3: 3a, 3b, 3c, 6, 9, 12

Top

Color 1: 1, 5, 9

Color 2: 2, 6, 10

Color 3: 3, 7, 11

Color 4: 4, 8, 12

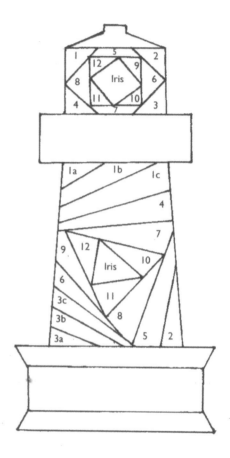

After completing the *Iris Folding*, tape a piece of holographic paper over the back side of both 'iris' openings. Cut the base, roof, and middle trim out of cardstock and adhere to the front side of the card. The fire flies were made using a hand punch.

42

Cross

Color 1: 1, 3, 5, 7, 8, 9, 10, 15, 16, 17, 18, 23, 24, 25, 26

Color 2: 2, 4, 6, 11, 12, 13, 14, 19, 20, 21, 22, 27, 28, 29, 30

I made this cross using two colors. You could use only one color. Just follow the sequence of numbers.

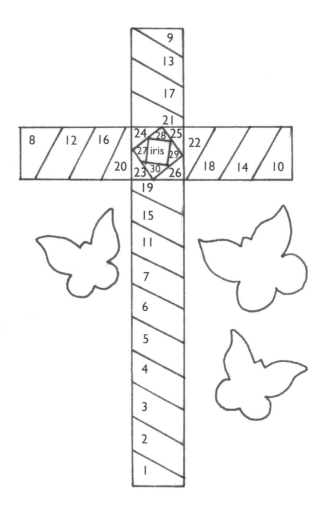

After completing the *Iris Folding*, tape a piece of holographic paper over the back side of the 'iris' opening. Cut the doves out of pearl colored paper and adhere to the front side of the card.

Cup Cake

Color 1: 1a, 1b, 1c, 1d, 5, 9, 13, 17

Color 2: 2a, 2b, 6, 10, 14, 18

Color 3: 3, 7, 11, 15, 19

Color 4: 4a, 4b, 4c, 4d, 8, 12, 16

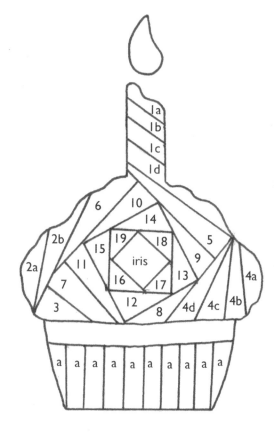

After completing the *Iris Folding*, tape a piece of holographic paper over the back side of the 'iris' opening. Cut the flame and brown trim out of cardstock and adhere to the front side of the card. The balloons were made using the Balloons pattern.

Purse and Glove

Color 1: 1, 4, 7, 10, 13, 16

Color 2: 2a, 2b, 2c, 2d, 5, 8, 11, 14, 17

Color 3: 3a, 3b, 3c, 6, 9, 12, 15, 18

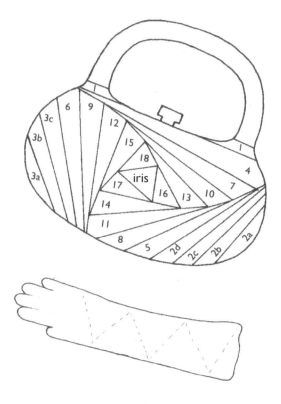

After completing the *Iris Folding*, tape a piece of holographic paper over the back side of the 'iris' opening. Cut the handle and clasp out of cardstock and adhere to the front side of the card. Cut the gloves out of white or printed paper and adhere to front of the card. The circles were made using a circle punch.

48

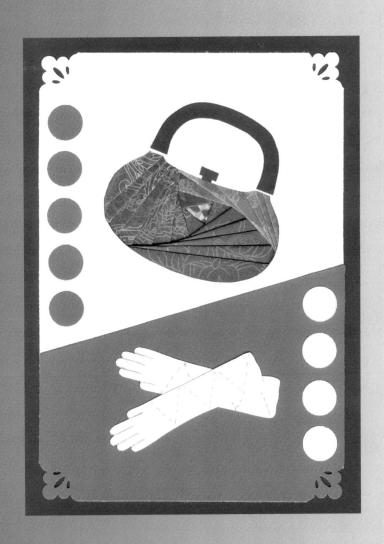

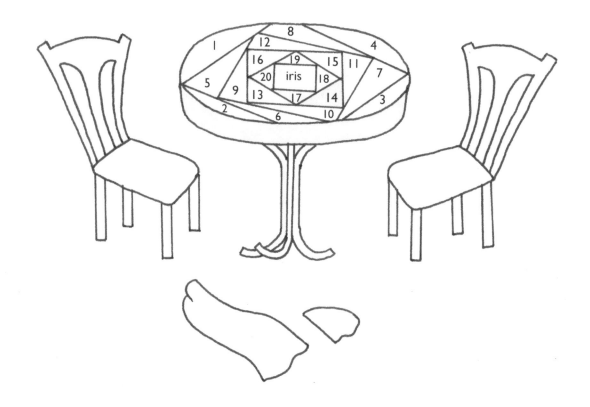

Table and Chairs

Color 1: 1, 5, 9, 13, 17
Color 2: 2, 6, 10, 14, 18
Color 3: 3, 7, 11, 15, 19
Color 4: 4, 8, 12, 16, 20

I used only two colors in this design. Color 1 & 3 are the same and color 2 & 4 are the same.

After completing the *Iris Folding*, tape a piece of holographic paper over the back side of the 'iris' opening. Cut the chairs, table side, legs, and towel out of cardstock and adhere to the front side of the card. Note that the towel goes on after the chair has been adhered. The butterflies were made using a hand punch.

Egg and Chicken

Top of Egg

Color 1: 1a, 1b, 1c, 4, 7

Color 2: 2, 5, 8

Color 3: 3a, 3b, 3c, 6, 9

Bottom of Egg

Color 1: 1a, 1b, 4, 7, 10, 13

Color 2: 2a, 2b, 5, 8, 11, 14

Color 3: 3, 6, 9, 12, 15

After completing the *Iris Folding*, tape a piece of holographic paper over the back side of the 'iris' opening. Cut the chicken out of cardstock and adhere to the front side of the card. Cut a small triangle for the beak. The grass and flowers were made using hand punches. They could easily be cut out by hand.

Wreath

This was made using one color. Follow the sequence of numbers.

Cut a piece of cardstock that matches the cardstock you are using and tape it to the back of the 'iris' opening. If you prefer, tape a photo instead.

Cut the bow out of cardstock and adhere to the front side of the card.

The trees and snowflakes were made using hand punches. The bird and berries were purchased stickers.

Angel

Color 1: 1, 4, 7, 10

Color 2: 2a, 2b, 5, 8, 11

Color 3: 3a, 3b, 6, 9, 12

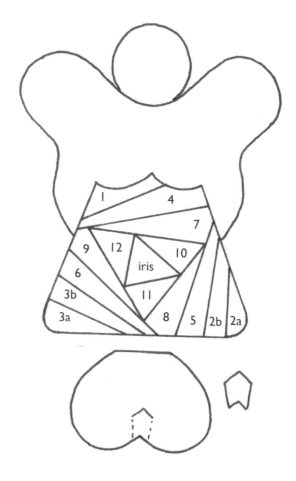

After completing the *Iris Folding,* tape a piece of holographic paper over the back side of the 'iris' opening.   Cut the wings, head, arms and hands out of cardstock and adhere to the front side of the card. Adhere in this order: wings first, arms second, hands third and head fourth. The halo was drawn on using a gold fine tipped pen.

Lamp Post

Color 1: 1, 5, 9, 13, 17, 21

Color 2: 2, 6, 10, 14, 18, 22

Color 3: 3, 7, 11, 15, 19, 23

Color 4: 4, 8, 12, 16, 20

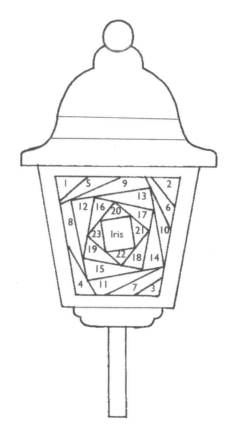

After completing the *Iris Folding*, tape a piece of holographic paper over the back side of the 'iris' opening.   Cut the roof, ball, base and pole out of cardstock and adhere to the front side of the card.   The fire flies were made using hand punches.

Making Your Own Patterns
Using Two Basic Templates

It is so easy to make your own patterns, using the templates that I have included on the next two pages. You don't need to be an artist! You only need the outline of a design, in which you cut out of cardstock. Then it's layered on top of the template. At this time, you are ready for *Iris Folding*. The illustration below shows how to use the templates. I have provided you with 12 outlines to help get you started. You could also use outlines from coloring books or free public domain clip art. It's that simple.

Look at your outline and determine if it is closer to a square or a triangle. After cutting your outline out of cardstock, layer it on top of one of the templates, focusing on centering the 'iris' within your aperture opening. Rotate the aperture until you find a position that looks good. Tape the template and aperture down using masking tape. Only iris fold the main body of your pattern. The other parts should be cut out of cardstock and adhered to the front side of your card. You are ready to *Iris Fold*.

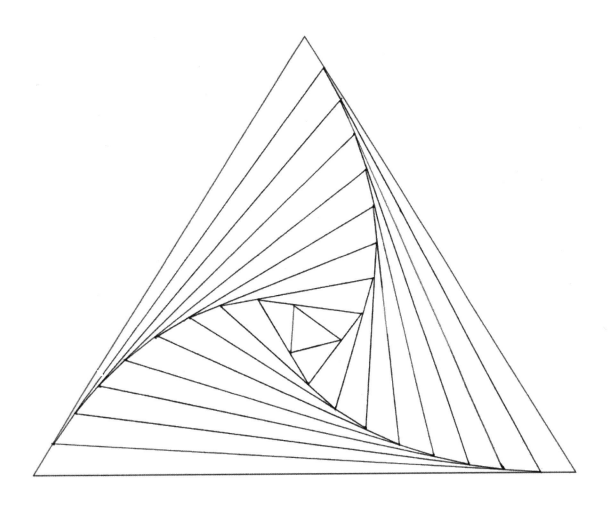

61

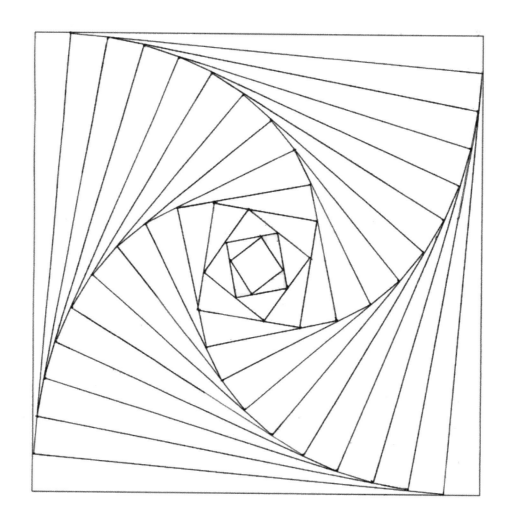

62

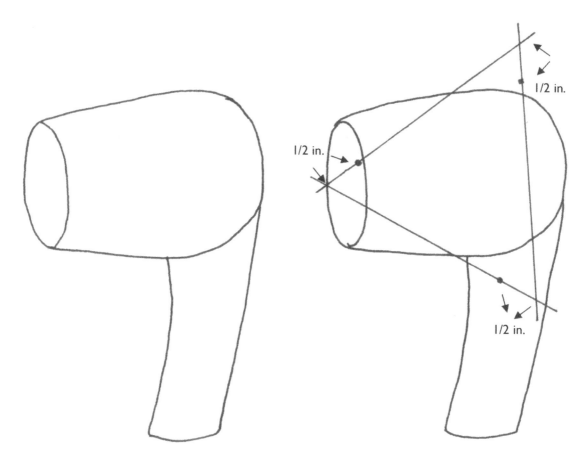

1/2 in.

1/2 in.

1/2 in.

Making Your Own Templates

Start by sketching the pattern that you desire (only the outline). Deciding that the blow dryer followed a triangular shape, I used a triangle to start my template. Note that I am not *Iris Folding* the handle or tip of the dryer. If your pattern is more like a square, then use a square. A square will produce a four color pattern. The triangle will produce a three color pattern. The instructions will be the same. Measure a 1/2 inch to the right from each corner and place a dot.

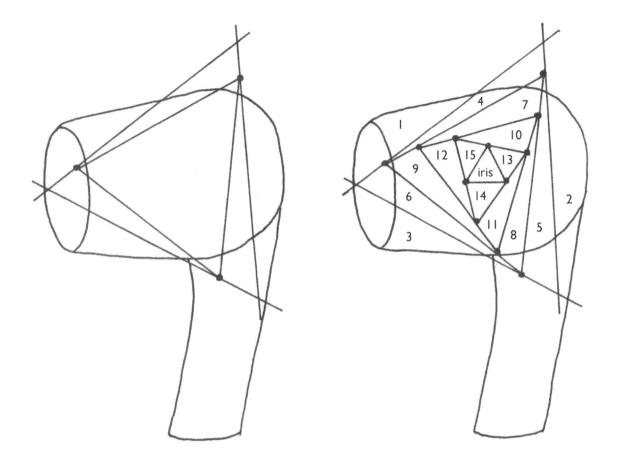

Draw a line from one dot to another, creating another triangle. Measure a 1/2 inch to the right from the corners of the new triangle. Once again, draw lines connecting the dots, creating another triangle. Continue doing this until you get close to the center of your design. You will always leave an opening in the center, creating the 'iris'. Erase any lines that extend beyond your *Iris Folding* area. In this case, it would be all lines on the handle and the tip of the blow dryer. Now you are ready to number your template. Notice that you have three sides to work from. You will be working from the outer part and moving inward. Start with side one and number 1. Move to side two and number 2. Move to side three and number 3. Keep spiraling around the template until you reach the inner part of your design. You are now ready to iris fold!

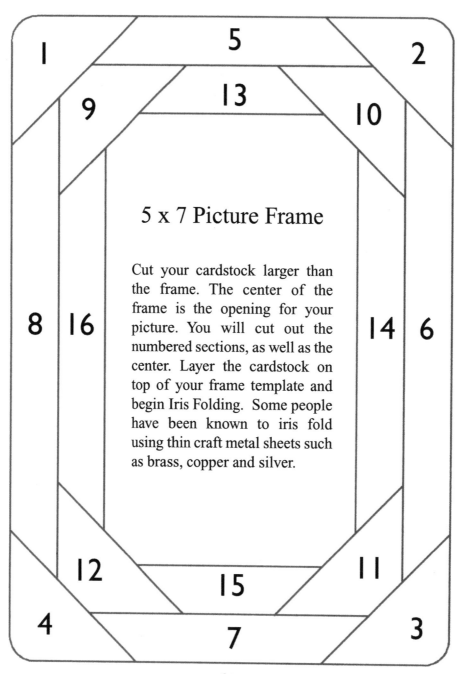

5 x 7 Picture Frame

Cut your cardstock larger than the frame. The center of the frame is the opening for your picture. You will cut out the numbered sections, as well as the center. Layer the cardstock on top of your frame template and begin Iris Folding. Some people have been known to iris fold using thin craft metal sheets such as brass, copper and silver.

Another year
older and more
experienced!

Happy Birthday

An apple a day
keeps the doctor
away. Hope you're
feeling better soon.

Wanted to let
you know how much
you're missed.

God had plans for
you before you
were born.
Believe that he
has great
things in store
for you!

Always
remember,
you're as young
as you feel!

Happy Birthday

This is your
one day to
wish.
Wish BIG!

We won't
count the candles!

Happy Birthday

Birthdays aren't
for remembering your
age, they're
a reminder that God
brought a wonderful
person into this world.

You only
celebrate
birthdays
once a year,
so make it good!

Do not throw away your confidence; it will be richly rewarded.
Hebrews 10:35

It's been wonderful having you as my 'secret sister'.

A true friend is someone who is there for you when they'd rather be anywhere else.
author unknown

Everything is possible for him who believes.
Mark 9:23

Best wishes on your new job promotion!

Congratulations on your 25th wedding anniversary.

May your wedding day be the beginning of a lifetime of happiness.

Congratulations on your 50th wedding anniversary.

May this holiday season bring you joy, peace and happiness!

I love you
Dad!

Happy Fathers
Day

**You're
like a sister
to me.
I love you.**

The difficulties in
life are intended to
make us better, not
bitter.
Author unknown

**I really
appreciate you, Mom.**

**Happy Mother's
Day**

**May you
be blessed
during this
holiday
season.**

**Your kindness
is so much
appreciated!**

**My life is
complete with
you in it!**

I was blessed
having a sister
like you!

**I cherish
our moments
together.**

Babies are a blessing
from God.

Congratulations!

**May you
find happiness
today and
always.**

God
understands our
prayers, even when
we can't find the
words to say them.
author unknown

**Your friendship
has made a
big difference in
my life.**

**May your
special day be
filled with
wonderful
moments.**

**Congratulations
on your new
arrival.**

**All your
dreams will come
true if you
have the courage to
pursue them.**

Wishing you
all the luck in the
world!

This is your day.
Enjoy every minute
of it!

Acknowledgements

I want to thank the following people:

Bill, my husband, for being there for me and recognizing that I have talent that should be shared with others.

BJ Page, my closest friend, for having faith in me and giving me the support I needed to make this dream come true. Thanks also, for critiquing my book and testing my instructions and patterns to assure that they are easily understood.

LaVergne, TN USA
08 November 2010
204048LV00002B